Daily Affirmations

Included in this journal should be repeated three times per day until you can repeat them from memory.

I have all the strength and confidence within me that I need to succeed

This Journal Belongs to:

___

COMMUNICATION LOG

DATE:

Today we spoke and I feel:

Today we didn't speak and I feel:

Today I received a package and I feel:

Today, I didn't receive a package and I feel:

"NO ONE IS YOU, THAT IS YOUR POWER"

REFLECTIONS

DATE:

"ANYTHING WORTH HAVING TAKES TIME."

REFLECTIONS

DATE:

"ANYTHING WORTH HAVING TAKES TIME."

REFLECTIONS

DATE:

"ANYTHING WORTH HAVING TAKES TIME."

COMMUNICATION LOG

DATE:

Today we spoke and I feel:

Today we didn't speak and I feel:

Today I received a package and I feel:

Today, I didn't receive a package and I feel:

"NO ONE IS YOU, THAT IS YOUR POWER"

REFLECTIONS

DATE:

"ANYTHING WORTH HAVING TAKES TIME."

REFLECTIONS

DATE:

"ANYTHING WORTH HAVING TAKES TIME."

REFLECTIONS

DATE:

"ANYTHING WORTH HAVING TAKES TIME."

REFLECTIONS

DATE:

"ANYTHING WORTH HAVING TAKES TIME."

I am in
control of
my life.

COMMUNICATION LOG

DATE:

Today we spoke and I feel:

Today we didn't speak and I feel:

Today I received a package and I feel:

Today, I didn't receive a package and I feel:

"NO ONE IS YOU, THAT IS YOUR POWER"

REFLECTIONS

DATE:

"ANYTHING WORTH HAVING TAKES TIME."

REFLECTIONS

DATE:

"ANYTHING WORTH HAVING TAKES TIME."

REFLECTIONS

DATE:

"ANYTHING WORTH HAVING TAKES TIME."

COMMUNICATION LOG

DATE:

Today we spoke and I feel:

Today we didn't speak and I feel:

Today I received a package and I feel:

Today, I didn't receive a package and I feel:

"NO ONE IS YOU, THAT IS YOUR POWER"

REFLECTIONS

DATE:

"ANYTHING WORTH HAVING TAKES TIME."

REFLECTIONS

DATE:

"ANYTHING WORTH HAVING TAKES TIME."

REFLECTIONS

DATE:

"ANYTHING WORTH HAVING TAKES TIME."

REFLECTIONS

DATE:

"ANYTHING WORTH HAVING TAKES TIME."

Today will be
a great day.

COMMUNICATION LOG

DATE:

Today we spoke and I feel:

Today we didn't speak and I feel:

Today I received a package and I feel:

Today, I didn't receive a package and I feel:

"NO ONE IS YOU, THAT IS YOUR POWER"

REFLECTIONS

DATE:

"ANYTHING WORTH HAVING TAKES TIME."

REFLECTIONS

DATE:

"ANYTHING WORTH HAVING TAKES TIME."

REFLECTIONS

DATE:

"ANYTHING WORTH HAVING TAKES TIME."

COMMUNICATION LOG

DATE:

Today we spoke and I feel:

Today we didn't speak and I feel:

Today I received a package and I feel:

Today, I didn't receive a package and I feel:

"NO ONE IS YOU, THAT IS YOUR POWER"

REFLECTIONS

DATE:

"ANYTHING WORTH HAVING TAKES TIME."

REFLECTIONS

DATE:

"ANYTHING WORTH HAVING TAKES TIME."

REFLECTIONS

DATE:

"ANYTHING WORTH HAVING TAKES TIME."

REFLECTIONS

DATE:

"ANYTHING WORTH HAVING TAKES TIME."

I am
awesome.

COMMUNICATION LOG

DATE:

Today we spoke and I feel:

Today we didn't speak and I feel:

Today I received a package and I feel:

Today, I didn't receive a package and I feel:

"NO ONE IS YOU, THAT IS YOUR POWER"

REFLECTIONS

DATE:

"ANYTHING WORTH HAVING TAKES TIME."

REFLECTIONS

DATE:

"ANYTHING WORTH HAVING TAKES TIME."

REFLECTIONS

DATE:

"ANYTHING WORTH HAVING TAKES TIME."

COMMUNICATION LOG

DATE:

Today we spoke and I feel:	Today we didn't speak and I feel:
Today I received a package and I feel:	Today, I didn't receive a package and I feel:

"NO ONE IS YOU, THAT IS YOUR POWER"

REFLECTIONS

DATE:

"ANYTHING WORTH HAVING TAKES TIME."

REFLECTIONS

DATE:

"ANYTHING WORTH HAVING TAKES TIME."

REFLECTIONS

DATE:

"ANYTHING WORTH HAVING TAKES TIME."

REFLECTIONS

DATE:

"ANYTHING WORTH HAVING TAKES TIME."

Nothing can
stop me
from
achieving
what I want

COMMUNICATION LOG

DATE:

Today we spoke and I feel:

Today we didn't speak and I feel:

Today I received a package and I feel:

Today, I didn't receive a package and I feel:

"NO ONE IS YOU, THAT IS YOUR POWER"

REFLECTIONS

DATE:

"ANYTHING WORTH HAVING TAKES TIME."

REFLECTIONS

DATE:

"ANYTHING WORTH HAVING TAKES TIME."

REFLECTIONS

DATE:

"ANYTHING WORTH HAVING TAKES TIME."

COMMUNICATION LOG

DATE:

Today we spoke and I feel:

Today we didn't speak and I feel:

Today I received a package and I feel:

Today, I didn't receive a package and I feel:

"NO ONE IS YOU, THAT IS YOUR POWER"

REFLECTIONS

DATE:

"ANYTHING WORTH HAVING TAKES TIME."

REFLECTIONS

DATE:

"ANYTHING WORTH HAVING TAKES TIME."

REFLECTIONS

DATE:

"ANYTHING WORTH HAVING TAKES TIME."

REFLECTIONS

DATE:

"ANYTHING WORTH HAVING TAKES TIME."

I can handle anything that comes my way.

COMMUNICATION LOG

DATE:

Today we spoke and I feel:

Today we didn't speak and I feel:

Today I received a package and I feel:

Today, I didn't receive a package and I feel:

"NO ONE IS YOU, THAT IS YOUR POWER"

REFLECTIONS

DATE:

"ANYTHING WORTH HAVING TAKES TIME."

REFLECTIONS

DATE:

"ANYTHING WORTH HAVING TAKES TIME."

REFLECTIONS

DATE:

"ANYTHING WORTH HAVING TAKES TIME."

COMMUNICATION LOG

DATE:

Today we spoke and I feel:

Today we didn't speak and I feel:

Today I received a package and I feel:

Today, I didn't receive a package and I feel:

"NO ONE IS YOU, THAT IS YOUR POWER"

REFLECTIONS

DATE:

"ANYTHING WORTH HAVING TAKES TIME."

REFLECTIONS

DATE:

"ANYTHING WORTH HAVING TAKES TIME."

REFLECTIONS

DATE:

"ANYTHING WORTH HAVING TAKES TIME."

REFLECTIONS

DATE:

"ANYTHING WORTH HAVING TAKES TIME."

I chose faith
over fear.

COMMUNICATION LOG

DATE:

Today we spoke and I feel:

Today we didn't speak and I feel:

Today I received a package and I feel:

Today, I didn't receive a package and I feel:

"NO ONE IS YOU, THAT IS YOUR POWER"

REFLECTIONS

DATE:

"ANYTHING WORTH HAVING TAKES TIME."

REFLECTIONS

DATE:

"ANYTHING WORTH HAVING TAKES TIME."

REFLECTIONS

DATE:

"ANYTHING WORTH HAVING TAKES TIME."

COMMUNICATION LOG

DATE:

Today we spoke and I feel:

Today we didn't speak and I feel:

Today I received a package and I feel:

Today, I didn't receive a package and I feel:

"NO ONE IS YOU, THAT IS YOUR POWER"

REFLECTIONS

DATE:

"ANYTHING WORTH HAVING TAKES TIME."

REFLECTIONS

DATE:

"ANYTHING WORTH HAVING TAKES TIME."

REFLECTIONS

DATE:

"ANYTHING WORTH HAVING TAKES TIME."

REFLECTIONS

DATE:

"ANYTHING WORTH HAVING TAKES TIME."

I'm willing to see things differently.

COMMUNICATION LOG

DATE:

Today we spoke and I feel:

Today we didn't speak and I feel:

Today I received a package and I feel:

Today, I didn't receive a package and I feel:

"NO ONE IS YOU, THAT IS YOUR POWER"

REFLECTIONS

DATE:

"ANYTHING WORTH HAVING TAKES TIME."

REFLECTIONS

DATE:

"ANYTHING WORTH HAVING TAKES TIME."

REFLECTIONS

DATE:

"ANYTHING WORTH HAVING TAKES TIME."

COMMUNICATION LOG

DATE:

Today we spoke and I feel:

Today we didn't speak and I feel:

Today I received a package and I feel:

Today, I didn't receive a package and I feel:

"NO ONE IS YOU, THAT IS YOUR POWER"

REFLECTIONS

DATE:

"ANYTHING WORTH HAVING TAKES TIME."

REFLECTIONS

DATE:

"ANYTHING WORTH HAVING TAKES TIME."

REFLECTIONS

DATE:

"ANYTHING WORTH HAVING TAKES TIME."

REFLECTIONS

DATE:

"ANYTHING WORTH HAVING TAKES TIME."

Everything
in life
happens for
me.

COMMUNICATION LOG

DATE:

Today we spoke and I feel:

Today we didn't speak and I feel:

Today I received a package and I feel:

Today, I didn't receive a package and I feel:

"NO ONE IS YOU, THAT IS YOUR POWER"

REFLECTIONS

DATE:

"ANYTHING WORTH HAVING TAKES TIME."

REFLECTIONS

DATE:

"ANYTHING WORTH HAVING TAKES TIME."

REFLECTIONS

DATE:

"ANYTHING WORTH HAVING TAKES TIME."

COMMUNICATION LOG

DATE:

Today we spoke and I feel:

Today we didn't speak and I feel:

Today I received a package and I feel:

Today, I didn't receive a package and I feel:

"NO ONE IS YOU, THAT IS YOUR POWER"

REFLECTIONS

DATE:

"ANYTHING WORTH HAVING TAKES TIME."

REFLECTIONS

DATE:

"ANYTHING WORTH HAVING TAKES TIME."

REFLECTIONS

DATE:

"ANYTHING WORTH HAVING TAKES TIME."

REFLECTIONS

DATE:

"ANYTHING WORTH HAVING TAKES TIME."

I will make
today count.

COMMUNICATION LOG

DATE:

Today we spoke and I feel:

Today we didn't speak and I feel:

Today I received a package and I feel:

Today, I didn't receive a package and I feel:

"NO ONE IS YOU, THAT IS YOUR POWER"

REFLECTIONS

DATE:

"ANYTHING WORTH HAVING TAKES TIME."

REFLECTIONS

DATE:

"ANYTHING WORTH HAVING TAKES TIME."

REFLECTIONS

DATE:

"ANYTHING WORTH HAVING TAKES TIME."

REFLECTIONS

DATE:

"ANYTHING WORTH HAVING TAKES TIME."

REFLECTIONS

DATE:

"ANYTHING WORTH HAVING TAKES TIME."

REFLECTIONS

DATE:

"ANYTHING WORTH HAVING TAKES TIME."

www.ingramcontent.com/pod-product-compliance
Ingram Content Group UK Ltd.
Pitfield, Milton Keynes, MK11 3LW, UK
UKHW040559210726
13854UKWH00008B/1525

9 781794 809192